Henry Guy Carleton

The Thompson Street Poker Club

Henry Guy Carleton

The Thompson Street Poker Club

ISBN/EAN: 9783337055950

Printed in Europe, USA, Canada, Australia, Japan

Cover: Foto ©Thomas Meinert / pixelio.de

More available books at **www.hansebooks.com**

THE
THOMPSON STREET
POKER CLUB

"YEZZAH—FO' ACES, AN' I DONE RASSLE WIF DAT NIGGAH WIF HE FO'
NINES TWELL HE DRAP MORE 'N A DOLLAH 'N FOHTY CENTS,"

THE
THOMPSON STREET
POKER CLUB

FROM

"L I F E"

———

ILLUSTRATED

———

NEW YORK:
WHITE AND ALLEN,
1888.

TO

THAT NOBLE EXPOUNDER OF THE GAME,

ROBERT C. SCHENCK,

These few reminiscences of blind, straddle, raise and draw are affectionately and yet cautiously dedicated, by

THE AUTHOR.

New York,
   April 16th, 1884.

POKER AMONG THE POETS.

♦♦♦

" Thou shalt lie down with kings."—*Thanatopsis.*

*   *   *   *

" I would give all my fame for a pot."—*Henry I .*

*   *   *   *

" Now might I do it pat."—*Hamlet.*

*   *   *   *

" I cannot draw."—*Lear.*

*   *   *   *

" Straight let us seek."—*King John.*

*   *   *   *

" Beware of entrance into a " [jack-pot] " but, being in, bear t that the opposed may beware of thee."—*Hamlet.*

*   *   *   *

' O for the touch of a vanished hand."— *Tennyson.*

TWO JACKS AN' A RAZZER.

THE REMARKABLE AND SUCCESSFUL HAND HELD BY MR. WILLIAMS.

THE Thompson Street Poker Club was in session, and a big jack-pot had been opened. There were evidently big hands out, for the bets and excitement ran high.

"Looker hyar, Gus, whuffer yo' rise dat pot!" exclaimed Mr. Tooter Williams.

"Nebber yo' mine! Yo' call, ef you is n't 'fraid; yes, yo' call—dat 's all!" retorted Gus, sullenly.

"I won't call! I rise you back," said Mr. Williams, whose vertebræ were ascending.

"I rise yo' ag'in," retorted Gus. And so they went at each other until chips, money, and collateral were gone. Mr. Williams concluded to call.

"Whad yo' got, nigger, dat yo' do all dat risin' on? Whad yo' got, nohow?" Gus laid down his hand—ace, king, queen, jack, and ten of clubs.

"Is dat good?" he inquired, beginning to size up the pot.

"TWO JACKS 'N' A RAZZER."

"No, dat's not good?" said Mr. WILLIAMS, reaching down in his boot-leg.

"Whad yo' got den?" queried GUS. Mr. WILLIAMS looked at him fixedly.

" Ise jes' got two jacks 'n' a razzer."

" Dat's good," said GUS.

The game then proceeded.

DAT'S GOOD!

MR. SMITH IS NOT TO BE BLUFFED WITH IMPUNITY

MR. TOOTER WILLIAMS astonished the Thompson Street Poker Club Saturday night by raising Mr. GUS JOHNSON sixty-five cents when that gentleman opened the last jack-pot of the evening. Mr. JOHNSON showed up two small pair and precipitately fell out; but the Rev. Mr. THANKFUL SMITH stood the raise and drew four cards. Mr. WILLIAMS stood pat. After the draw Mr. SMITH skinned his cards, breathed very hard and bet a postage stamp and a battered cent. Mr. WILLIAMS promptly raised him a dollar and forty cents. Mr. SMITH hesitated, but finally drew forth his wallet. "Look hyar, yo' coon, what yo' got dat yo'se gittin' so brash?"

" Yo' fine out ef yo' bet dat dollah fohty—jes' yo' see," retorted Mr. WILLIAMS, evidently getting excited.

"Yo'se done rise de tar outen me too offen. Now what yo' got?" said the Rev. Mr. SMITH, putting his money into the pot.

Mr. WILLIAMS looked disconcerted. "I—I'se jes' got a small king full," he faltered.

"I HAIN'T GOT NUFFIN'."

"King full's good," said the Rev. Mr. SMITH.

"But I aint got it," said Mr. WILLIAMS.

"What has yo' got den?" said the Rev. Mr. SMITH.

"I'se got three queens."

"Three queens is good," said the Rev. Mr. SMITH.

"But I haint got 'em," said Mr. WILLIAMS.

"What has yo' got, den?" queried the Rev. Mr. SMITH, growing a little impatient.

"I'se got two par," said Mr. WILLIAMS.

"Dat's good," said the Rev. Mr. SMITH.

"But I haint got 'em."

"Oh, come now, nigger, what has yo' got?"

"I'se got one par.

"*Dat's* good."

"But I haint got it," said Mr. WILLIAMS, whose situation was growing perilous.

"Lans' stars, nigger, quit yo' foolin'! What *has* yo' got?"

Mr. WILLIAMS slowly skinned his cards. "I—I haint got nuffin'."

"WELL, DAT 'S GOOD !"

WHAR 'S DE CASH FER DESE BEANS?

THE REV. MR. THANKFUL SMITH HAS TROUBLE WITH THE BANK.

OWING to the unfortunate fact that the chips loaned to the Thompson Street Poker Club by Mr. RUBE JACKSON had been garnisheed by Mr. GUS JOHNSON (see Rule 147, which provides for the payment of I. O. U.'s), the members present last Saturday evening were compelled to play with beans—a limited quantity of which had been thoughtfully secured by the Rev. Mr. THANKFUL SMITH while passing a produce store in the late afternoon.

The cards ran well, and as Mr. SMITH himself was responsible for the bank, the betting was unusually brilliant. Mr. SMITH was never in better luck, nor Mr. TOOTER WILLIAMS in worse. Notwithstanding the heavy losses of the latter gentleman, however, the supply of beans seemed never to run short, and after several hours of play this excited suspicion in the banker.

"Lemme jess cash up and see how de bank stan's," said that potentate, after an unusually prodigal burst of beans from Mr. WILLIAMS had startled the players.

Mr. GUS JOHNSON passed in ninety-six beans and got his money.

Professor BRICK had thirty-nine lentils and a half; but consented, after some haggling, to call it plain thirty-nine.

Mr. RUBE JACKSON had seventy-two beans, but owed the bank seventy-five. He settled the difference with coin. All accounts had now been squared except that of Mr. WILLIAMS.

The Rev. Mr. SMITH emptied the beans into his hat, put the pack into his pocket, and made away with the stuffed wallet. Every eye was fixed on Mr. WILLIAMS.

"Look hyar, niggah! whar's de cash fer dese beans?" asked that gentleman of the banker.

By way of reply Mr. SMITH emptied the bank upon the table and desired the Committee of the Whole to count it. The return was nine hundred and seventy-two beans. Then said Mr. SMITH, impressively:

"I only had fo' hundred an' sixty beans ter start; I 'se winned all de jackers and mos' ob de stray tussels, an' yet I 'se a dollah fohty-two out. Dis bank 's solven' as long 's de bettin' 's squar'; but de debbil himse'f caw'nt cash agin de man wat 's got a umbreller-case full o' beans dribblin' from his sleeve. *No*, sah! Dis bank am 'spended."

The Club adjourned.

A NIGGAH FUNER'L.

THERE was no game at the Thompson Street Poker Club on Saturday evening. Mr. GUS JOHNSON was engaged to sing at a revival in Hoboken; Professor BRICK wrote a note to the effect that his coal man had prevented his recuperating sufficiently to play on the cash system; and Mr. RUBE JACKSON, who had promised to call upon Elder Boss JONES, of Florida, and steer him against the game, failed to put in an appearance.

"WHAR'S DE CASH FO' DEM BEANS?"

The Rev. THANKFUL SMITH was relating the experiences of the previous meeting, when, with the saddened air of a man who had lost his grip on his reputation, Mr. TOOTER WILLIAMS and the odor of a Bowery cigar entered together.

"Whad de madder, Toot?" inquired Mr. SMITH with the easy familiarity of a man in luck.   "Yo' looks 'spondent."

"I done loss dat sixty-fo' dollahs I winned on de hoss race," responded Mr. WILLIAMS gloomily.

"Sho!" exclaimed everybody present.

"Yezzah," continued Mr. WILLIAMS, addressing himself exclusively to Mr. SMITH, "an' I done loss it in bettin' agin' mokes, too. *Dat's* whad makes de remorse bite."

The deepest interest having been aroused, Mr. WILLIAMS proceeded to enlighten the members as follows :

" I was stannin' in a do' on Sixth Aveyou, an' up comes a wite man in a plug hat, an' sezee, 'Why *heel*-lo, Mister ROBIN-son, how is yo'?' "

"Bunko," remarked Mr. SMITH, with the air of one who had had experience.

"Dat's what *I* thought," said Mr. WILLIAMS, "bud I kept shet. So I sez to him, 'How is yo'?'"

"'I'se a stranger yar, Mister ROBINSON,' sezee, 'an' I mus' say I never did see so many mokes togidder as dey is on Sixth Aveyou. Dey's mo' mokes dan wite pussons.' 'Oh no,' sez I, 'dey's mo' wite pussons dan mokes.' 'I'll bet yo' two to one dey isn't,' sezee. 'All right,' sez I. So off he goes an' comes back wid a fren' who weighed 'bout two hunded, an' had a bad eye."

"Yo' had a sof' spec," observed Mr. SMITH.

"Den," continued Mr. WILLIAMS, not noticing the inter-ruption, "sezee, 'Now, we'll bofe put up a hunded dollahs wif dis genelman, an' stan yar in de do'. Every wite man passes, he'll give yo' two dollahs, an' every moke passes, he'll give *me* a dollah.'"

"A NIGGAH FUNER'L."

"Well!" said Mr. SMITH, who was growing excited.

"Well ! fust dey comes along two wite men, and de man wif de bad eye says dat was fo' dollahs to my credit. Den comes six wite men an' he say dat 's twelve dollahs mo' for me. Den comes along a buck niggah and den I lose a dollah. Den fo' wite men an' I win eight. Den fo' wite men mo'; den one niggah ; den two niggahs, den seven wite men, and de man wif de bad eye, he say I was fohty-two dollahs ahead."

"De soffes' lay I ever hear," said Mr. SMITH, whose eyes were glistening over Mr. WILLIAMS' winnings.

"Den comes along fo' wite men," said Mr. WILLIAMS, "an' de man wif a bad eye he say dat was eight dollahs mo', an' *den*——" here Mr. WILLIAMS paused, as if his recollections had overpowered him.

"An' den ?" echoed everybody, wildly excited.

"Why, den," said Mr. WILLIAMS, desperately, " dey comes around de cornah——"

"De cops ?" breathlessly asked Mr. SMITH.

"A niggah funer'l," said Mr. WILLIAMS.

" I BROKE YO' ALL UP."

THE regular monthly meeting of the Thompson Street Poker Club occurred last Saturday evening, and as Mr. RUBE JACKSON had succeeded in steering the Reverend Dr. JEFF COOPPULLER against the game, the members were in high spirits.

Under Section 5, Rule IV., visitors and guests are allowed to settle with the bank at the end of the game, and in accordance with this hospitable privilege, the reverend gentleman had drawn so heavily as to make Mr. GUS JOHNSON's eyes stand out like a crab's with excitement.

Mr. TOOTER WILLIAMS was in luck. It had been already

"I BROKE YO' ALL UP."

secretly remarked by older members of the Club that whenever the Club played with an old pack, Mr. WILLIAMS' luck was invariably steadier and more brilliant, but on this occasion it rose to such majestic proportions that every one but the Club's guest fled precipitately on his slightest symptom of showing fight, and the battle was mainly between these two.

The Rev. THANKFUL SMITH was banking, as usual. He honored his reverend friend's cal' for chips with cheerfulness and alacrity for four straight hours. Then Mr. WILLIAMS pleaded an engagement, passed in his toppling pile, and received $14, even, which was the biggest winning on the Club's record. He then left.

The Rev. Dr. COOPPULLER made another liberal draft on the bank, and began losing to Mr. GUS JOHNSON. The Rev. Mr. SMITH was beginning to have his suspicions. At last he said :

"Sposen we jess cash in, an' squar wid de bank."

Mr. GUS JOHNSON handed in his winnings and received $3.41.

Mr. RUBE JACKSON owed the bank 92 cents, and paid it with a trade-dollar. All eyes were now fixed upon the guest of the evening.

"Yo' owes de bank, brudder, 'bout $19.79," said Mr. SMITH, with an effort to be calm.

"Dat's all right," said Mr. COOPPULLER, putting on his gloves.

"Wha—whad's all right?" inquired Mr. SMITH, who was beginning to realize the worst.

"Dat $19.79," answered Mr. COOPPULLER, drawing on his coat.

"Whar's de cash?" inquired Mr. SMITH.

"Yo' gin it ter Toot, did n' yo'?" asked Mr. COOPPULLER.

"He winned it!" asseverated Mr. SMITH.

"Dat's not my fault," said Mr. COOPPULLER.

"I broke yo' all up, ef yo' doan squar dat 'count," said Mr. SMITH, shucking off his coat and assuming a terrible position.

Mr. COOPPULLER smiled. "I was jess—jess foolin', brudder. Yar 's a check fo' twenty-fo' dollahs. Gin me de change."

"Mr. SMITH counted out four dollars and twenty-one cents, and shook hands with Mr. COOPPULLER, who beamed with a benevolence only exceeded by the caution with which he smuggled a wink to Mr. RUBE JACKSON. Then he and that gentleman left together. There was silence. Mr. GUS JOHNSON was examining the cheque. He handed it back to Mr. SMITH with a smile.

"Dat 's all right?" asked Mr. SMITH.

"All right; 'ceptin'—"

"'Ceptin' whad?"

"Dat bank busted mo 'n a y'ar ago."

"DAT BANK BUSTED MO' N A YAR AGO."

THE SCRAPED TRAY.

MR. TOOTER WILLIAMS was late at the meeting of the Thompson Street Poker Club, Saturday evening ; but as he had Elder Boss DICKERSON in tow, the secretary remitted the usual fine.   It was confidentially learned that the Elder had just received $17.50 on an extensive kalsomining contract, and was probably good for as much more, and as Mr. WILLIAMS had already played with the deck of cards now upon the table, and Mr. RUBE JACKSON had consented for a small percentage not to play, but to sit in a sociable way behind the Elder's chair, the game promised to be one of extraordinary interest.

Having been introduced to the Rev. Mr. THANKFUL SMITH, Mr. GUS JOHNSON and Professor BRICK, the Elder shucked off his ulster, produced a corpulent wallet, purchased $1.79 worth of blues and red, and opened up the game with an expression of determination and a thumping blind, which made the excitable Mr. JOHNSON's eyes stand out like those of an apoplectic crab. Seven hands were played, and as Mr. JACKSON, who sat behind the Elder, had evidently forgotten the code of signals to the extent that he winked with his right eye when he should have winked with his left, Mr. WILLIAMS was already out ninety-seven cents, and was correspondingly mad.

At last, however, Mr. JACKSON was made aware of his error by a searching kick delivered beneath the table, and a new deck, which had been thoughtfully placed on ice by the Rev. Mr. SMITH before the company assembled, was produced. It was Mr. JOHNSON's deal, and the Elder's blind.

Everybody came in.

The Elder raised the blind 65 cents.

The decisive moment had come.

"I rise dat rise a dollah," said the Rev. THANKFUL SMITH, with the calmness of one who expects to fill a bobtail.

"I sees yo' dat, and I liff yo' a dollah mo'," ventured Mr. WILLIAMS.

"I calls," said the Elder.

Mr. SMITH also called, and the three proceeded to draw cards. Mr. WILLIAMS wanted two cards; the Rev. Mr. SMITH guessed he 'd take one, and the Elder concluded to play what he had.

Mr. SMITH led out with a two dollar stack. Mr. WILLIAMS slowly pulled out a corpulent wallet, fixed a belligerent glare apparently on Mr. SMITH, banged the wallet heavily on the middle of the table, and said, impressively :

"I goes yo' dat two, an' six dollahs rise."

"I rise yo' six," said the Elder, but without putting up chips.

The Rev. Mr. Smith dropped out. Mr. WILLIAMS pointed to the wallet, and said :

"I goes yo' six mo'."

The Elder raised one foot, and placed it neatly on top of Mr. WILLIAMS' wallet, and said :

"I rise dat ten."

"Whar 's de money?" inquired Mr. WILLIAMS, with a polite smile.

"Whar 's yo' money?" retorted the Elder, as sweetly.

Mr. WILLIAMS pointed to the wallet underneath the Elder's heel.

" Dat 's all right, den," said the Elder ; " I 'se got jess as much leather on dis yar table as yo' has."

" Whad yo' mean by dat ?" asked Mr. WILLIAMS.

" Put up er shet," said the Elder.

Mr. WILLIAMS drove his knife through his cards, pinning them to the table, and called out the Rev. Mr. SMITH for a consultation. The Elder thoughtfully whistled a tune, drew a razor, and seemed to be trying its edge on the surface of his bottom card. Mr. JACKSON watched Mr. WILLIAMS' hand to see that nothing got away, and Mr. JOHNSON kept his eye on the pack.

Mr. WILLIAMS returned triumphantly, and counted out thirty dollars, which he had evidently borrowed from Mr. SMITH.

" I calls," he said.

The Elder put up his razor, shook $29 out of his wallet, made up a dollar more with mutilated coin, some pennies and a postage-stamp, and said, briefly :

" Whad yo' got ?"

" Fo' kings," said Mr. WILLIAMS, with a deadly gleam in his eye.

" Not good," said the Elder.

" Wha—whad ?" faltered Mr. WILLIAMS.

" Fo' aces." With this the Elder showed four aces, swept the pot into his hat and left the room. The five sat dazed.

" I done guv him three aces an' two trays, sho," said Mr. JOHNSON.

" I put dat han' up mysef," asseverated Mr. SMITH, bewildered.

" I seed bofe dem trays in he hand," observed Mr. JACKSON.

Mr. WILLIAMS said nothing, but silently examined the Elder's hand. Finally he inquired, hoarsely :

" Did he hev a razzer ?"

"Yezzah," said Mr. JACKSON ; "he done play with he razzer de whole time yo' was outen de room."

Mr. WILLIAMS rose with a withering look, and put on his coat.

"Whad 's de matter, TOOT ?" inquired Mr. SMITH. "How yo' splain hit ?"

Mr. WILLIAMS pointed to the ace of diamonds, lately in the Elder's hand. "Gin any niggah de tray er diamonds an' a razzer an' tree aces, and whad kin fo' kings do ? Gwuffum heah. He done played me outen thirty dollars on er scraped tray. Dad 's what makes me 'spise pokah."

With this, Mr. WILLIAMS left the room.

DAT 'S GAMBLIN'.

AT the regular meeting of the Thompson Street Poker Club, on Saturday evening, owing to the fact that both his eyes had that morning accidentally collided with the knuckles of the Rev. Mr. THANKFUL SMITH, after a slight financial misunderstanding, and that for two hours he had lost every jackpot he had opened, Mr. TOOTER WILLIAMS presented somewhat the aspect of gloom. Mr. GUS JOHNSON was one dollar and forty-nine cents ahead, having had an unusually steady two-pair streak ; Mr. RUBE JACKSON had sixty-nine cents' worth of velvet before him ; Professor BRICK was a few coppers and a postage stamp on the right side ; and Mr. WILLIAMS, who was banking, was the only loser. It being his deal, three kings wandered into his hand, and might have proved

" DEM NINES 'LL WIN, SHO'."

effectual but for the sad fact that everybody noticed the expression of his eye and fled. A jack-pot was then in order, and after it had climbed to aces the players braced up and knew that the event of the evening hed come. At that moment the door opened and the Rev. Mr. SMITH, accompanied by a slight odor of hiccoughs, entered, took his seat behind Mr. JACKSON's chair, and glared a renewal of the morning's hostilities at Mr. WILLIAMS. That gentleman haughtily refused to notice it, however, but opened the pot with a burst of chips which scared Mr. JOHNSON half to death. Professor BRICK came in.

"Rise dat," said the Rev. Mr. SMITH to Mr. JACKSON. Then he whispered audibly : "Dem tree nines 'll win dat pot, sho."

Mr. JACKSON elevated the bet as directed. Mr. WILLIAMS was delighted, for he had three jacks. He returned the raise.

"Rise him agin," commanded the Rev. Mr. SMITH, and then whispered as before : "Doan leggo dem nines."

Back came Mr. WILLIAMS, and then the Rev. Mr. SMITH counseled Mr. JACKSON to "jess call," and "and see what dem nines 'll ketch in the draw."

Mr. JACKSON wanted two cards, and caught a pair of trays. Mr. WILLIAMS held up a king and drew one card, which, after elaborately combing his hand, he discovered to be another king. The battle was then resumed.

"I 'll back dem nines for all I'se wuff," said Mr. SMITH, slipping his wallet into Mr. JACKSON's hand. And so they went at each other until even Mr. WILLIAMS' new collar button was up, and he was forced to call:

"What yo' got, niggah?"

"Whad yo' got yo'se'f?" retorted Mr. JACKSON.

"I'se got er jack-full—*dat's* what *I* got," said Mr. WILLIAMS.

"Shome down," said Mr. SMITH, imperturbably.

Mr. WILLIAMS proudly skinned out three jacks and a pair of kings, and inquired rather superciliously, was "dat good?"

"We'se loaded fer bar over yar," retorted Mr. SMITH, evasively.

"Whad?" asked Mr. WILLIAMS, astonished; for, as dealer, he was certain he had not given Mr. WILLIAMS a fourth nine.

"We'se jess—jess loaded fer bar."

"Whad's dat?" reiterated Mr. WILLIAMS, turning as pale as he could. "Shope dem nines!"

Mr. SMITH's only reply was to spread Mr. JACKSON's hand out. It consisted mainly of queens, with a flavor of trays to give it strength. He then gathered in the pot and, with Mr. JACKSON, quitted the room. Mr. WILLIAMS sat in deep thought. After a little he said: "I like de game for fun—jess, jess to pass away de time. But *dat*"—here Mr. WILLIAMS waved his hand towards the débris of the recent encounter, with the air of one inculcating a lofty moral—"dat 's gamblin'!"

"WHAD YO' CUT?"

DAR 'S NO SUCKAHS IN HOBOKEN.

THE INCOMPREHENSIBLE DEMEANOR OF MR. DILSEY.

FOR three weeks, until last Saturday, the Thompson Street POKER CLUB had had no session. This was partly due to the fact that the proprietor of the building had sordidly closed the room and kicked Mr. GUS JOHNSON, the treasurer, down stairs on learning that, owing to some inexplicable phenomenon not understood by the Club, the kitty had not yielded enough to pay for the kerosene, much less the rent.

As a regular rake on two pairs and upward had been made, for a month, this delinquency amazed the Club. Various scientific theories were advanced, among them one involving a search of Mr. JOHNSON's private pocket and bootleg, but investigation had shown them to be false. An inspection of the table-drawer was then made. It was shown that a knot-hole existed in the bottom thereof, large enough to admit of the insertion of two fingers or the abstraction of three dollars, which was the amount of the missing kitty. It was also demonstrated that the knot-hole had been in perihelion, so to speak, with Mr.

Tooter Williams.   Therefore, while it was clear that the money was hopelessly gone, it was impossible to account for its absence upon any other theory than that offered by Mr. Williams himself that de mice done smell dat las' welch rahbit offen Mr. Johnson's fingahs on de bills, an' run off wid it." This explanation was received in lieu of a better ; the Rev. Mr. Thankful Smith paid the rent and assumed charge of the kitty until he should be reimbursed ; Mr. Johnson magnanimously forgave the gentleman who had kicked him down-stairs.   Mr. Tooter Williams expressed his belief in Mr. Johnson's integrity as Treasurer, and all was again harmony

Mr. Cyanide Whiffles, for a moderate percentage, had volunteered to steer his brother-in-law against the game, and, to use a technical expression, blow him in for all he was worth. The gentleman in question was a Hoboken barber with a steady income, a total ignorance of draw-poker, a child-like confidence and other advantages of mind and person which impressed Mr. Williams favorably.

The Rev. Mr. Smith instructed the neophyte in those fundamental principles known as " coming in," " straddling," " rising," and " sweetnin' de jacker," and by tacit consent he was allowed to win some small successive pots and thus got himself into a glorious humor.   Then Mr. Williams winked at Gus Johnson, and that gentleman dealt.

Mr. Williams had straddled the blind and the Rev. Mr. Smith straddled him.   All came in, and drew three cards apiece except the stranger, Mr. Highland Dilsey, who only wanted one.   Mr Williams bet a dollar.   Mr. Smith raised him two.

Professor Brick called, as did also Mr. Whiffles.   All eyes were upon Mr. Dilsey, and the silence was so profound that Mr. Johnson could hear his hair grow.

"Does yo' jess—jess call, Mistah Dilsey," inquired Mr. Williams, with a sweet smile, " or does yo' rise it ?"

Mr DILSEY passed his cards in review, hesitated, and said:
"Kin I rise it?"

"Certainly," replied Mr. WILLIAMS, who had a great deal
of benevolence and also three kings. "Rise it all yo' want."

Thus encouraged, Mr. DILSEY raised the pot six dollars.
Everybody breathed hard with suppressed excitement, and Mr
JOHNSON's eyes might have served for a hat rack. Mr. WIL-
LIAMS raised back and Mr. SMITH raised him. The others, ac-
cording to previous agreement, fled.

Mr. DILSEY called. "What yo' got to beat two par?" he
inquired.

"Is sev'ral big, fat, smilin' kings any good?" asked Mr.
WILLIAMS kindly.

"Kin a spade flisk, queen high, do nuffin'?" queried the
Rev. Mr. SMITH.

"Shome up," said Mr. DILSEY, apparently nursing his left
foot.

Mr. WILLIAMS unfolded his private collection of royalty,
and Mr. SMITH exhibited a panorama of spades which reflected
great credit upon Mr. JOHNSON's dealing.

"I 'se sorry, Mistah DILSEY," observed Mr. WILLIAMS.

"Dat 's de way wif cyards," remarked the Rev. Mr. SMITH,
sententiously. "Gamblin' 's onsartin."

Mr. DILSEY spoke not, but began to count up the pot.

"Wha—whad yo' doin' wif de spondles?" asked Mr. WIL-
LIAMS.

"Leggo my pot!" commanded Mr. SMITH.

Mr. DILSEY coolly rolled up the bills and inserted them in
an abyss under his vest, and then swept the coppers and Mr.
WHIFFLES' plated watch-chain into his pocket.

"Look hyar, niggahs," he said, in a tone which made Mr.
JOHNSON feel like a refrigerator, "I 'se from Hoboken, an' I 'se
a barbah. When a Hoboken barbah comes to Thoms'n Street,
he kerries his profession wif him. I 'se got bofe boot-legs an'

"DAR 'S NO SUCKAHS IN HOBOKEN."

a hip-pocket full er de implements ob de craff.   Yo' hear me ?"

All signified by silence that they heard. Then Mr. DILSEY laid down three jacks and a pair of sixes, and coolly jammed Mr. WHIFFLES' hat down over his eyes and quitted the room.

The Club sat stricken for three minutes.   Then the door slowly reopened, and Mr. DILSEY's voice sounded sepulchrally:

" Dar 's no suckahs in Hoboken."

With that he vanished.

DE SEVEN CENTS.

PROCEEDS OF AN ENTERTAINMENT FOR THE BARTHOLDI
PEDESTAL FUND.

A SPECIAL meeting of the Thompson Street Poker Club was held last Saturday evening for the purpose of discussing the ways and means of aiding the Bartholdi Pedestal Fund.   Mr. TOOTER WILLIAMS, who had unfortunately not entirely recovered from an acute attack of malaria contracted on New Year's Day, was found to be too unparliamentary and uproarious to occupy the Chair, so that power was conferred upon the Rev. Mr. THANKFUL SMITH, who, though evidently convalescing from the same malady, was drowsy but dignified, and banked as usual.

Mr. RUBE JACKSON opened the question and the jack-pot by remarking that he had seen a photograph of the statue, and thought that its complexion should strongly recommend it to the zeal of the colored race.

Mr. GUS. JOHNSON passed out with the remark that he never did n't have no luck on jackers nohow, and wanted to hear the

Bartholdi matter more fully discussed before venturing an opinion.

Mr. CYANIDE WHIFFLES came in without remark.

Mr. TOOTER WILLIAMS woke up and said he would open the pot for a dollar and a half. Mr. RUBE JACKSON, who saw there was trouble coming, hastened to mildly assure him it had already been opened for thirty-five cents. Then said Mr. WILLIAMS in a voice of war :

"I rise dat two dollahs, 'n I 'll knock de tar outen de niggah wot doan' rassle."

This definite proposition had the effect of scaring Mr. JACKSON half to death, and of recalling the Rev. Mr. SMITH from the temporary state of coma into which he had lapsed. He drowsily ran over his hand, inquired who had opened the pot, and on being informed of Mr. WILLIAMS' belligerent burst of chips, electrified all present by drawing forth the honorable wallet and slapping it on the table with great violence. He then said to Mr. WILLIAMS :

"Look hyar, TOOT ; what yo' doin ?"

"I jess—jess rised dat pot," faltered Mr. WILLIAMS, who had not forgotten past experiences with that wallet.

"Yo' *rised* it, did yer ?" sarcastically inquired Mr. SMITH : "*yo'* rised it ?" Here he opened the wallet and shook out a roll of bills. "I see dat rise 'n I swole dat pot ten, twonny— —fohty dollahs." Here he leaned back and smiled reassuringly on Mr. JACKSON, who had begun to breathe again.

Mr. WILLIAMS ran his hand over. It somehow did n't seem to be as large as before. He then said :

"I—I 'sidered dis pot was fer—fer de fun'."

"Wot fun' ?" asked Mr. SMITH.

" De pedestal fun' ?"

" Dat 's why you swole de jacker ?"

"Ye—yes."

"BRER JACKSON 'LL TAKE DE SEBEN CENTS."

"Well, den, for de sake ob de pedestal fun', I jess swole it fohty dollahs."

Mr. WILLIAMS respiration was labored for a few minutes, during which time he ran his hand over again.

"I'se a patriot," he said, "an' I 'll do anyt'ing in de cause."

"Den yo' call dat rise?"

Mr. WILLIAMS threw up his hand. The Rev. Mr. SMITH raked in the jack, counted it over twice, and said :

"De gross proceeds of dis entertainment am five dollahs 'n seventy-two cents. Five from thirteen, nine, carry one ; six 'n four 's nine—dat leaves jis seven cents profit fer de fun'. Brudder Jackson will take charge ob de seven cents," he concluded, passing that sum over in coppers.

"Bud whar—whar 's de res' ob de money goin'," inquired Mr. WILLIAMS.

"The res' of de money," said Mr. SMITH, impressively, " is absorbed by de 'spenses ob de entertainment. Brudder JACK-SON will now pass around de aces."

TRIFLIN' WIF PROV'DENCE.

THE Thompson Street Poker Club met as usual last Saturday evening, the Rev. Mr. THANKFUL SMITH in the chair. There were present Professor BRICK, Mr. CYANIDE WHIFFLES and Elder JUBILEE ANDERSON, whom Mr. TOOTER WILLIAMS, as an act of courtesy, had volunteered to steer against the game. A note of regrets was received from Mr. GUS. JOHNSON. Owing to a slight misunderstanding in relation to the ownership of an overcoat, he had a temporary engagement with the municipal authorities.

The game was spirited, the jack-pots frequent and exciting, and the luck for two hours ran steadily against the Elder.

Mr. TOOTER WILLIAMS had been to a stag dinner in the early evening, and the heating influence of the maccaroni compelled him about every fifth hand to seek the outer air and cool himself. Each time he returned, however, he would indulge in such a reckless burst of chips and flushes as to mislead his guest into the supposition that it would be wiser for him to go home and sleep it off. But as he steadily won it was useless to make the proposition.

At eleven o'clock the Elder had lost six dollars and drew out of the game. Mr. WILLIAMS was nine dollars and Mr. WHIFFLES' ulster ahead. The Rev. Mr. SMITH was gloomy and Professor BRICK seemed to be deliberating what form of suicide would be cheapest and most effective. Mr. WILLIAMS, from being musically uproarious, had become incoherent and abusive. He drew three cards against Mr. WHIFFLES' pat flush and got him four dollars in debt, and he bounced the Rev. Mr. SMITH out of a jack-pot with two miserable fives, which he gleefully showed down. He was then again attacked by maccaroni and vanished for a breath of fresh air.

"Kin I play yo' han', Toot?" inquired the Elder, as Mr. WILLIAMS rose.

"Cern'ly," replied that gentleman. "An' when yo' ketch 'em, kyarve Smith—kyarve 'im!" With two lurches and this truculent request, he quitted the room.

The Elder smiled across at the Rev. Mr. SMITH, and that gentleman winked at Mr. WHIFFLES, who dealt.

"I bets yo' a dollah," observed the Elder.

"I rises dat fo'," retorted the Rev. Mr. SMITH.

"I calls. Gimme a cyard," said the Elder.

"Me too," said the Rev. Mr. SMITH.

"Fo' dol'ahs," said the Elder, making a cavern in Mr. WILLIAMS's pile.

"Fo' mo'," said the Rev. Mr. SMITH.

At that moment a door slammed, and Mr. WHIFFLES knew that trouble and Mr. WILLIAMS was coming.

"Fo' mo 'n yo'," was the Elder's reply, as he shoved up the last of Mr. WILLIAMS' chips and Mr. WHIFFLES' ulster.

"Rise dat fo'," replied the Rev. Mr. SMITH. At that moment Mr. WILLIAMS entered. His practised eye took in the situation at once.

"Wha—whadjer doin'?" he asked the Elder.

"Playin' yo' han'," replied that gentleman, giving him the cards.

"Who—who done all dat risin'?" was Mr. WILLIAMS' next inquiry.

"HE TRIED ON MR. WHIFFLES' ULSTER."

"*I* did ; *dad's* who,' said the Rev. Mr. SMITH.

Mr. WILLIAMS ran his hand over. It held two trays, a pair of nines, and a king.

"Spose—sposen I rise yo' back ?" he said to the Rev. Mr. SMITH, in tones which he hoped would fill him with terror.

" Rise away," was that gentleman's imperturbable reply.

Mr. WILLIAMS, for a moment, was plunged in profound thought. Then he threw up his hand. The Elder slowly drew in the pot, buried it in his pocket, tried the fit of Mr. WHIFFLES' ulster, found it too small, gave it back to its owner, and then with the Elder and a somewhat fiendish chuckle, quitted the room. There was silence for a minute, and then Mr. WILLIAMS said, impressively :

" Niggas, *dad's* what er genelman gits for takin' his eye offen de pack. Dad speeyunce done cos' me jess—jess six dollahs a minit—dat fresh air was jess sixty cents a breff, while I was outen de room. Dad 's not pokah. Dad 's triflin wif prov'dence."

"WHARJER GIT DEM JACKS?"

MR. WILLIAMS AND MR. SMITH HAVE A SLIGHT MISUNDER-
STANDING.

M R. TOOTER WILLIAMS had a bad eye and several kings when the Rev. Mr. THANKFUL SMITH opened the first jack-pot at the regular meeting of the Thompson Street Poker Club, Saturday evening. Mr. GUS JOHNSON saw that a powerful brew of mischief was at hand, and prudently laid down two pair ; while Mr. CYANIDE WHIFFLES, who had a severe cold, a pair of eights, and very little horse sense, came in.

"I rise dat two dollahs," said Mr. WILLIAMS, quietly, but with truculence of intent.

"Yo's gittin' too brash," rejoined the Rev. Mr. SMITH, testily. "Ef yo' tinks yo' 's de Vandybilk er dis pahty, jess—jess stack 'em up. I rise yo' six dollahs."

Mr. WILLIAMS considered for a moment, during which time he thoughtfully examined the cards which with great foresight he had previously pinned to the leg of the table.

"I calls," he said, at length. "Gimme two cyards."

Mr. WHIFFLES fled.

The Rev. Mr. SMITH dealt Mr. WILLIAMS two cards, and conscientiously helped himself to the last ten-spot remaining in the pack. He then banged the honored wallet on the table and said :

"'Leven dollahs."

"I calls yo'," said Mr. WILLIAMS, secretly unpinning the hidden hand, and counting out the money.

The Rev. Mr. SMITH swept the pot into his pocket.

"Wha—whadjer doin'?" gasped Mr. WILLIAMS, aghast at this unparliamentary proceeding.

"Fo' tens," said the Rev. Mr. SMITH, showing down that remarkable hand. "How many freckles yo' got on yo' han'?" he inquired.

"I'se—I'se jess—jess clum over yo' tens," said Mr. WILLIAMS, with an effort to be calm and look honest.

"Shome up," said the reverend gentleman.

Mr. WILLIAMS unfolded four jacks. They were all there.

"Wharjer get um?" was the next point in the Rev. Mr. SMITH's catechism.

"Outen de pack, er course," said Mr. WILLIAMS, breathing hard.

The Rev. Mr. SMITH's reply was to reach over and weave his fingers firmly through the roots of Mr. WILLIAMS' hair. Then he thrashed around the room with him for a few excited

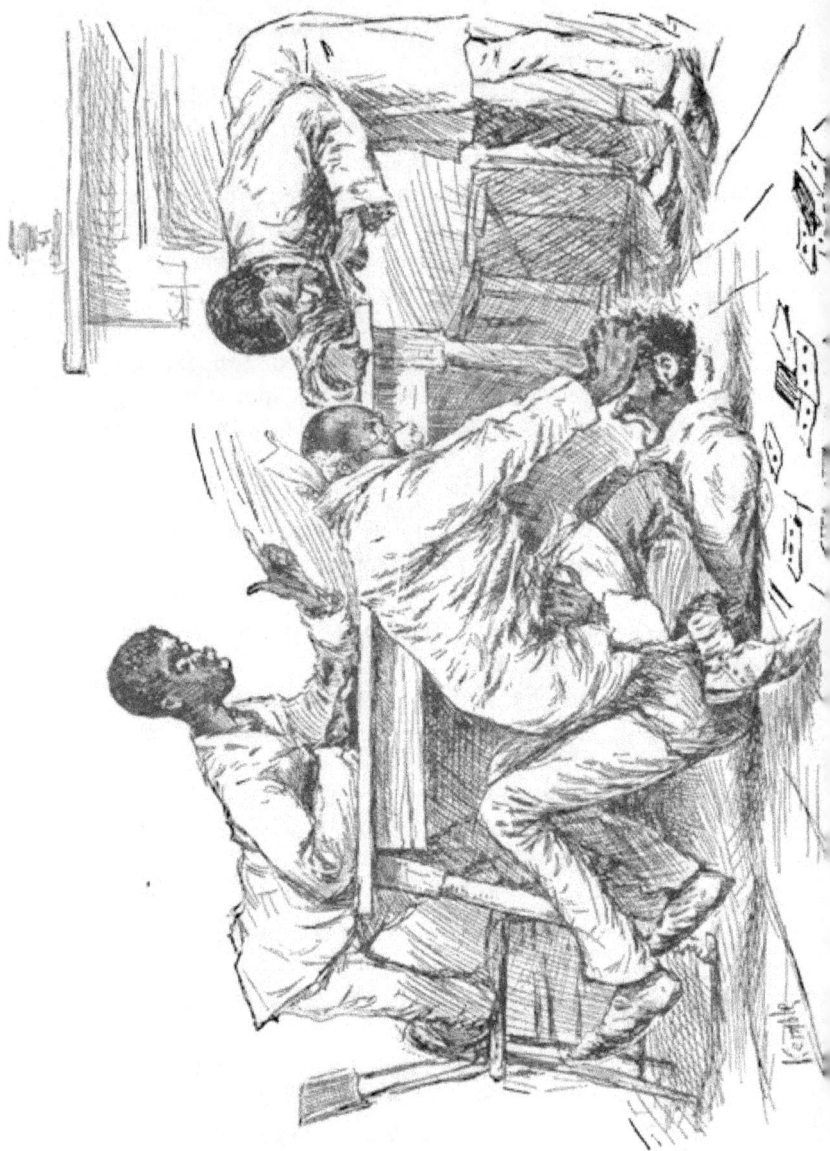

minutes and then sat down upon him. Mr. WILLIAMS still breathed heavily.

"Wharjer git dem jacks?"

"Outen de pack," again responded Mr. WILLIAMS, making a feeble effort to get up.

The Rev. Mr. SMITH butted his head nineteen times against the floor with great rapidity and violence, and again inquired, softly :

"Wharjer gettum?"

"Outen de pack. Leggo my kinks," urged Mr. WILLIAMS, still breathing heavily. Again his head was butted violently against the floor until the landlord on the floor above was impressed with the idea that the Club was refreshing itself with a solo on the bass drum.

"Whar—jer—git—dem—jacks?" inquired the Rev. Mr. SMITH, emphasising each word with a double butt.

"Outen—de—" here Mr. WILLIAMS faltered.

"Outen de what?" asked the Rev. Mr. SMITH with a temporary cessation of hostilities.

"De bug," said Mr. WILLIAMS, doggedly.   "Lemme up."

The Rev. Mr. SMITH unloaded himself from Mr. WILLIAMS's abdomen, arose, crossed the room and possessed himself of the extra cards pinned to the table.

"*Dis* whadjer call de *bug?*" he asked.

"Yezzah," said Mr. WILLIAMS, gloomy but respectful.

The Rev. Mr. SMITH assumed his overcoat. Then he replied to Mr. WILLIAMS :

"Toot, by the prowishuns of rule sixty-fo', yo' am suspended till de next meetin,' an' doan yo' work de bug no mo'-Mistah CYANIDE WHIFFLES an' GUS JOHNSON will now come down ter de s'loon an' rassle wif a sassenger an' some beer."

The Club then adjourned.

Mr. WILLIAMS breathed heavily.

"TROD SOF'LY, NIGGAHS."

MR. TOOTER WILLIAMS opened the first jack-pot with a little hesitation and four white chips, Saturday evening. Deacon TROTLINE ANGUISH, who had strayed in under the chaperonage of Mr. CYANIDE WHIFFLES, and who apparently had jacks-up and a very superficial knowledge of Mr. WILLIAMS, came in. Mr. RUBE JACKSON felt a strong temptation to put a plaster on the back of the wall-eyed king he had caught, hold him up with the deuces and try and pull something, but the studied indifference with which Mr. WILLIAMS gazed into space, made him lay down his hand and wish he were dead. Mr. CYANIDE WHIFFLES borrowed a blue chip from the Deacon "jess—jess till de nex' han'," and came in and kept the change. Then all eyes naturally centred on the Rev. Mr. THANKFUL SMITH, who, in addition to a barricade of chips which made Mr. WHIFFLES'S mouth water, had a four flush and a cheerfulness of demeanor which boded no good.

"Ez my fren' TOOT's done open dat jacker," he began, sweetly, "I rises hit." So saying, he put up such a stack of blue chips that Mr. WHIFFLES nearly fainted.

"Whad yo' go do dat for, Brer THANKFUL?" inquired the Deacon, in wild remonstrance. "Dat's not de speret ob de Gospil."

"Whar—whar yo' fin' draw-poker in de Gospil?" testily rejoined Mr. SMITH. "Does yo' tink de Possles 'n de 'Vangelists writ de Scripter after rasslin' wid a two-cyard draw agin a flush?" he sarcastically inquired. "*No*, Brer ANGUISH. Less ten' ter business. Dis ain't no prar meetin'—ceptin' Brer WILLIAMS seems to be on de anxious seat."

"Who—*who's* on de anxious seat?" asked Mr. WILLIAMS, hotly. "Yo' jess come on ; I rises yo' fo' dollahs."

The Deacon sadly ran over his hand. "De Gospil, Brer THANKFUL," he began ; "de Gospil."

"Cheese dat," said the Rev. Mr. SMITH. "Is yo' goin' ter pray or poke?"

"I'se gwine ter poke," he replied ; "I'se gwine ter see yo' rise" here he shoved up a stack of blues—"an' Brer TOOT s rise"—here he shoved up another stack—"an' I'se gwine ter rise it jess a leetle, 'cordin' ter de speret ob de good Book"— here he shoved up six dollars.

Mr. WHIFFLES fled.

Mr. JACKSON was breathing still, but that was all.

The Rev. Mr. SMITH glared defiance. "I rise yo' back."

"*I* rise *yo'*," said Mr. WILLIAMS.

"An' I rise TOOT," said the Deacon.

The Rev. Mr. SMITH was aghast. He was dealing, and knew by intuition that he would catch his fifth club ; but there was a serenity on the other side of the table which affrighted him.

"I jess—jess calls," he said.

"I calls," said Mr. WILLIAMS.

"Help de genelmen," said the Deacon, with the benevolence which invariably accompanies a pat hand.

Mr. WILLIAMS broke his two pair and drew to his jacks.

The Rev. Mr. SMITH got his club.

"Six dollahs," said the Deacon, after Mr. WILLIAMS had timidly ventured one chip.

"I calls," said the Rev. Mr. SMITH, sullenly

"I rise dat six mo'," said Mr WILLIAMS.

"I rise yo' six," said the Deacon.

"I calls," gasped Mr SMITH, shoving up his last chip and his snuff-box.

"Six mo'," said Mr. WILLIAMS.

"Six mo'," said the Deacon.

Mr. SMITH shucked off his overcoat and added to it his spectacles. "I calls," he said, as though speaking from the tomb.

"Six mo'," said Mr. WILLIAMS.

"Six mo'," said the Deacon.

"I—I hain't got nuffin' mo'," said the Rev. Mr. SMITH, faltering.

"Shove up dat watch," said Mr. WILLIAMS.

"Soak dem new boots," urged the Deacon.

"An' dat golhedded cane," suggested Mr. JACKSON, who, of course, however, had no business to speak, and was accordingly suppressed.

The Rev. Mr. SMITH hesitated. Then he sighed and threw up his hand. To his great astonishment Mr. WILLIAMS did the same. The elder softly hummed a hymn, tried the focal length of Mr. SMITH's spectacles, assumed Mr. SMITH's ulster, thoughtfully inserted Mr. SMITH's watch-chain in his vest-pocket, collared the bank and counted it, and then, with a cheerful smile at Mr. WILLIAMS, left the room. The silence for several minutes was sepulchral. Then Mr. JACKSON said:

"I 'se 'fraid——"

"Yo' 'se 'fraid ob what?" asked the Rev. Mr. SMITH, savagely.

"Dad TOOT 's played yo'."

"Wha—whad?" gasped Mr. SMITH.

"Dad was a sawbuck," said Mr. JACKSON.

"Whad 's a sawbuck?"

"TROD SOF'LY, NIGGAHS; TROD OUT SOF'LY."

"Why, dad pious niggah's Toot's cust fuzzin—Toot's dad's nevvy," said Mr. Jackson.

A light broke upon the Rev. Mr. Smith. "Dey was risin' an' risin—ter—ter knock de tar outen *me?*' he inquired, in a voice which froze Mr. Whiffles' marrow.

"Yezzah," said Mr. Jackson, keeping the table well between them.

Mr. Smith turned over Mr. Williams' hand. It contained two jacks. He examined the Deacon's. It held just three hearts, a spade and a club. He then re-examined his own flush. It was still perfect.

"Niggahs," he said, with the calmness of despair, "go out sof'ly, and lemme alone. I 'se been a prayin' and a-rasslin' wif Satan now gwine onto thutty-fo' yar, and dis am de fus' time I done got roped in by de combination er Gospil an' draw. Go out, sof'ly, niggahs." I want er rassle wif de dickshunary an' de angel ob wrath er while, an' den git de mos' feasible words an' club I kin fine, ter spress my feelin's ter Brer Toot and Brer Anguish. Trod sof'ly, niggahs—trod out sof'ly."

They trod.

"WHUFFER YO' RISE DAT?"

THE VERY EXTRAORDINARY HAND HELD BY MR. JOHNSON.

THE Thompson Street Poker Club had an unusually quiet game, with the luck steadily against Mr. Tooter Williams, until an unusually tough jack-pot brightened up the interest. Mr. Williams glanced across the table and saw the eyes of Mr. Gus Johnson shining with the light of something very big.

Mr. Williams passed.

Mr. Whiffles passed.

Mr. JOHNSON opened the pot with a defiant air and forty-six cents in mutilated coin.

The dealer, Mr. RUBE JACKSON, came in.

Mr. WILLIAMS promptly raised the bet two punched quarters and a ten-cent stamp.

"Whuffer yo' rise dat?" asked Mr. JOHNSON, whom this extraordinary action excited.

"Nebber yo' mine," said Mr. WILLIAMS, sullenly. "Jess yo' put up er shut up—dat's all.

"'Spose I'se got three jacks an' rise you back?" suggested Mr. JOHNSON.

"And 'spose I'se got a flisk, eh? Jess 'spose I's got a flisk, niggah; whar's yo' three jacks—eh?" Mr. WILLIAMS breathed very hard and glared at Mr. JOHNSON till even that gentleman's vest buttons were cold.

Mr. JOHNSON faltered, ran his hand over twice, sized up the pot, and decided he'd "jess call." They then proceeded to draw cards.

Mr. WILLIAMS thought he'd play what he had.

Mr. JOHNSON drew two cards to three tens and caught a pair of nines. This considerably reassured him. He bet thirty cents with the remark: "Now jess go ahead on dat flisk—jess fool away yo' substance much as yo' choose."

Mr. WILLIAMS thoughtfully raised him forty cents and a plug of tobacco.

Mr. JOHNSON saw the raise and retaliated by wagering a plated watch-guard and a pair of spectacles, borrowed from the Rev. THANKFUL SMITH who sat behind him.

Mr. WILLIAMS raised back. And so it went until there was nothing left to bet except the lamp and table, which were common property, inalienable under the constitution.

"Now, niggah," said Mr. WILLIAMS, "jess show down dem jacks."

"I haint got no jacks," said Mr. JOHNSON.   'I was lyin'.

I had three ten-speckers, befo' de draw. Show down yo' flisk ; dat 's what *I* want ter see."

"Well, I haint got no flisk," said Mr. WILLIAMS.

"What has yo' got? Show up yo' straight?" demanded Mr JOHNSON.

"Haint got no straight."

"Show up dat two par, den."

"Haint got no two par."

"What has yo' got, den, niggah?" Mr. JOHNSON was beginning to have his suspicions.

Mr. WILLIAMS slowly and triumphantly skinned out three jacks and a pair of trays. Mr. JOHNSON rose to leave the room.

"I doan mine losen my substance, an' I doan mine a squar' beat ; but I doan draw no mo' cyards agin a liar."

THE CLUB ADJOURNED.

www.ingramcontent.com/pod-product-compliance
Lightning Source LLC
Chambersburg PA
CBHW021555270326
41931CB00009B/1226